100 Classic Golf Tips
From Leading Ladies'
Teaching and Touring Pros

100 C
Golf

From Leading Ladies' Teaching and

Edited by *Christopher Obetz* with *Dave Allen*

Drawings by
Anthony Ravielli

Foreword by
Kathy Whitworth

lassic

Tips

ouring Pros

Scioto golf matriarchs, left to right: Corinne Redick (chairwoman 1973), Kay Licklider, Mary Obetz, and Jeanette Davis.

Dedicated to the memory of Mary Postlewaite "Gigi" Obetz, loving grandmother and mother to many golfers.

See you on another fairway, *Christopher*

Conte

nts

DURING MY PLAYING CAREER, I had the good fortune of getting to know many golf legends, including Patty Berg, Mickey Wright, Byron Nelson, and Ben Hogan.

While I only met Hogan a few times, each occasion was special. My favorite recollection of Hogan is at a dinner in New York in June 1988 celebrating the Centennial of Golf in America. Hogan was giving a speech and suddenly started talking about the grip. I was sitting between Arnold Palmer and Jack Nicklaus, and when I glanced underneath the table, both had joined their hands together as if holding an imaginary club, just as I and about everyone else in the room had. It was quite amusing but, at the same time, it underscored just how much respect we had for Hogan and his knowledge of the swing and the fundamentals.

Hogan has become synonymous with the grip, primarily because of the chapter he dedicates to this all-important fundamental in *Five Lessons: The Modern Fundamentals of Golf*. It's been more than fifty years since he wrote this classic instruction manual, and yet it remains one of golf's most popular books. I still find myself paging through it from time to time, not only for Hogan's explanations of the basics—which I find to be the true building blocks of any swing—but for the illustrations which accompany each lesson: the attention to detail and precision of Anthony Ravielli's drawings is truly fabulous. I couldn't be more delighted that

Rizzoli has found a way to celebrate Ravielli's work and the history of women's golf together in one book. In *100 Classic Golf Tips from Leading Ladies' Teaching and Touring Pros*, Ravielli's drawings walk you through more than six decades of women's golf, from the early days of Babe Zaharias and Louise Suggs to the modern swings of Annika Sorenstam and Lorena Ochoa. A compilation of timeless tips excerpted from the archives of *Golf Digest* and *Golf for Women* magazines, you'll find lessons from many of the greatest female players and teachers of all time, including Mickey Wright, Patty Berg, Peggy Kirk Bell, Nancy Lopez, Judy Rankin, Suggs, and Sorenstam.

When I turned professional in 1959, Mickey Wright was one of the first players I sought for advice. She was, in my mind, the best striker of the ball—man or woman—of that era, and while I knew right away that I could never hit the ball like she did, it gave me something to strive for. And I admired Patty Berg so much because she was a great ambassador for women's golf, and she taught me to become a more complete player. In 1961, I signed with Wilson Golf. As part of my duties, I had to conduct thirty to forty clinics a year, so Wilson had me join Berg for six weeks in the off-season to learn how. These exhibitions forced me to become a more versatile player. I learned how to shape shots, hit the ball high or low, and get out of all sorts of trouble. No longer did I have to wait for a golf course to be favorable to my style of play; I could adjust my game to whatever type of shot was needed. It was from that point on that my confidence and my play really took off. I hope that in reading this book, you'll not only gain a greater appreciation for the talents of these women, but you'll learn as much from them as I did in my forty-plus years of playing competitive golf.

As much as I learned from these great players, I would never have become the player that I did or the person that I am today without the tutelage of the great Harvey Penick, my teacher for nearly forty years. I will never forget my first day with him in Austin. I was almost seventeen, and the very first words out of his mouth were, "I think I can help you, but you've got to do what I tell you." That was Harvey. For three days we worked on nothing but getting my hands on the club correctly, and aim. Whenever he saw me change my grip, he would walk in and adjust my hands to the proper position. Harvey wouldn't let me get away with anything, and, for that, I'm so thankful.

In this book, I'm happy to share with you some of the lessons I've learned from Harvey and my playing days. As with all of the other tips and illustrations here, there is a great story behind each. Enjoy!

Kathy Whitworth, LPGA Hall of Famer

Kathy Whitworth's eighty-eight tournament wins are the most ever by a professional golfer, male or female. For more great tips from Kathy, see her book, *Kathy Whitworth's Little Book of Golf Wisdom: A Lifetime of Lessons from Golf's Winningest Pro.*

100 TIPS

1.Grip

01

PROPER LEFT-HAND GRIP ALLOWS HANDS TO WORK TOGETHER

Your index finger applies the most pressure

Whatever grip you use, it's best to get your left hand in correct position first. Here's a way to check for correctness. Lower your left hand to the club from above, not from underneath, and align the clubhandle across the palm and fingers so that the butt of the handle rests just under the heel of the hand. Then, close your index finger around the shaft and leave the rest of the fingers extended. This done, you should be able to pick the club directly upright with pressure from the index finger alone. The grip of the club fits snugly under the heel, and the index finger feels in control.

Kathy Whitworth

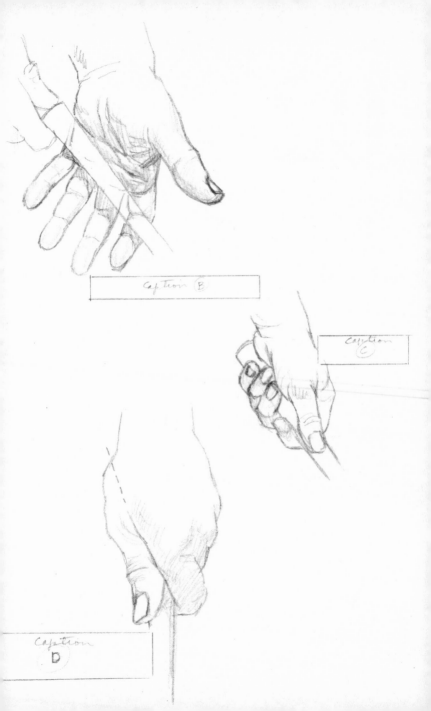

Caption B

Caption C

Caption D

02

TAKE A FIRM GRIP

*Avoid putting your hands
on too loosely*

The hands should not be tense,
but firm, so they will not shift position on the shaft.
This is one point ladies generally have trouble with
because of the lack of strength in the hands. Grip the
club so that it feels comfortable but still gives the
sensation of firmness. *Patty Berg*

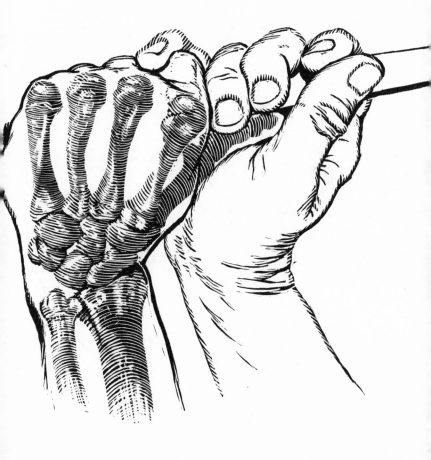

A. Ravielli

03

USE YOUR LIFELINE

*Cover your left thumb to
unify your grip*

For both feel and control you
want to hold the club in your fingers, not in your palm.
If you have to take the lid off a jar, do you hold it in your
fingers or palm? You instinctively grip it in your fingers
because that's where the strength and feel are, right?

A good way to ensure that your hands work
together is to grip the club so your left thumb fits along
the lifeline that runs along the pad of your right thumb.

Amy Alcott

04

SHAPE YOUR SHOTS

Adjust your grip pressure to fade or draw the ball

Whether your grip the club firmly or softly, it is important to keep your level of grip pressure constant throughout the swing. By varying a few pressure points, however, you can better shape your shots. For instance, if you want to hit a fade, grip the club a little bit tighter with the last three fingers of your left hand. And if you need a right-to-left trajectory, exert more pressure on the thumb and index finger of your right hand.

Make a few practice swings to get the feel of these pressure changes. Then set up and hit the shot as you would normally. Just hang on a little tighter with the right or left hand depending on what kind of shot is required. *Val Skinner*

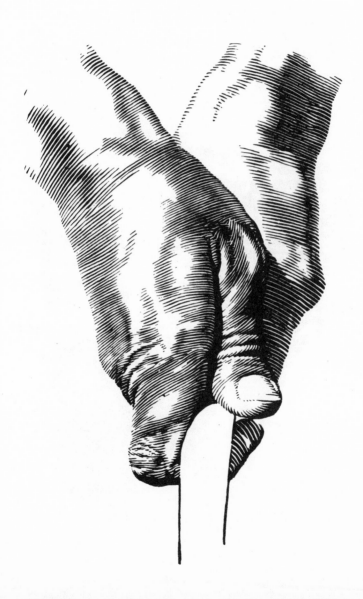

05

RIGHT-HAND GRIP

The club lies in your fingers, not in your palm

Throughout most of my amateur career I was never really comfortable with my grip. I wasn't getting a solid feel on my shots and I was losing distance with a fade that was very nearly a slice. During my freshman year at the University of Tulsa I went to see Buddy Phillips, head professional at the Cedar Ridge Country Club, and he gave me a lesson that I feel was a major reason for my success on the LPGA Tour.

With my old grip, the club laid almost in the palm of my right hand. When I opened the hand, the palm faced up to the sky. Buddy changed that, placing the club more in the fingers of my right hand. With the new grip, when I opened my hand if faced toward the target. I started hitting the ball much more solidly, with a slight draw. *Nancy Lopez*

06 GRIP STYLES

Interlocking, overlapping, or baseball—which one is for you?

The interlocking grip (bottom, left) is the grip I use, and I think it's an outstanding grip for women, juniors or anyone with small hands. I also think it's a good grip for people whose hands might be weakened by arthritis or other ailments. With this grip you actually interlock the little finger of your right hand with the forefinger of your left.

The overlapping or Vardon grip (top) is the most popular. With this grip, the little finger of your right hand rests on top of the notch formed between the index and middle fingers of your left hand. The final option is the baseball, or ten-finger grip (bottom, right). In this grip, your dominant hand usually takes over, preventing your hands from working as a unit. *Amy Alcott*

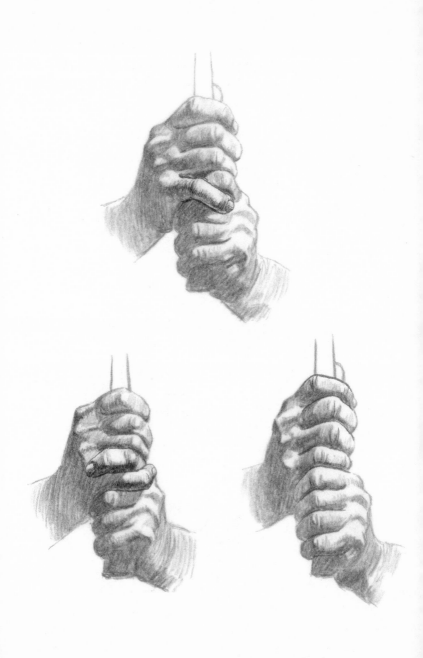

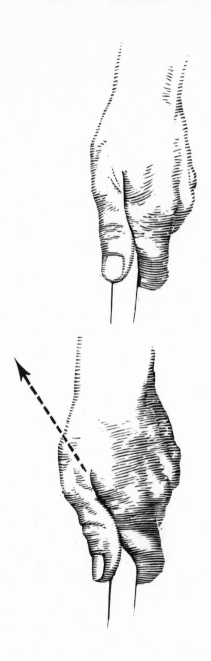

07

STRENGTHEN YOUR GRIP

Get 'Vs' to point toward right shoulder for greater distance

If you can afford to sacrifice some accuracy for more distance and/or you want to draw your shots (from right to left), try strengthening your grip. Place the left hand more on top of the club and the right hand underneath. The V's formed by your thumbs and forefingers point to your right shoulder. You should be able to see three or four knuckles of your left hand at address.

This position allows for greater wrist action in the swing and promotes an inside-to-outside swing path. The result usually is a lower trajectory, right-to-left curvature and more distance. ***DeDe Owens***

2.Setu

p

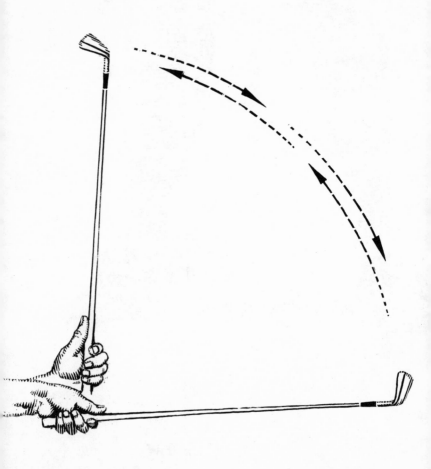

08

STORED ENERGY

Learn how to hinge and unhinge your wrists for maximum power

By allowing your wrists to hinge and unhinge, you create a lot more power while using a lot less energy. When you hinge your wrists, you're building and storing power. When you unhinge your wrists, you're releasing the pent-up power.

Here's a drill to help in the natural hinging and unhinging motion of your wrists. Take a mid-iron, tee up a ball, and set up as you normally do. Swing your arms back so your left arm is parallel to the ground. Make sure your wrists are hinged upward so your left thumb is pointing up and your arm and club are forming the letter "L." Now let your arms swing down and your wrists unhinge. After you hit the ball, your follow-through position should mirror your backswing. *Kathy Hart Wood*

09

GET ANCHORED

Push your feet against the ground to create a stable platform for your swing

My favorite tip for players of all levels to assure they strike the ball more solidly is to get well balanced and anchored at address. Set up with your head slightly behind the ball, within your own axis points or frame (you should feel tension on the insides of your thighs and your feet), and anchored to the ground. Literally push against the ground throughout the entire swing for power and centeredness. *Patti McGowan*

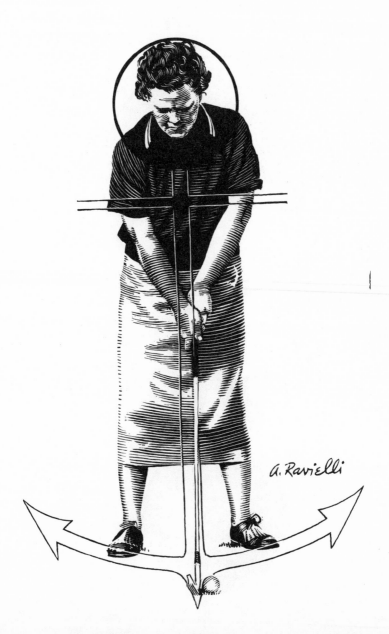

A. Ravielli

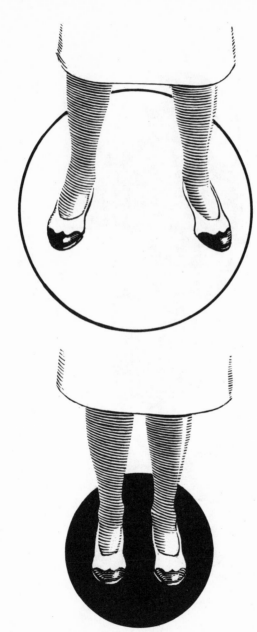

10

NARROW TRACKS

Bring your feet closer together to promote a bigger turn and more power

If a loss of flexibility is limiting your rotation and robbing you of distance, try narrowing your stance. This will allow you to turn your hips and shoulders farther in the backswing and the follow-through, adding power and length to your shots. To maintain stability, bend your knees a little more than you're used to and flare both feet slightly open (toes out) at address. *Kathy Whitworth*

11

ALIGNMENT CHECK

Look to your shoulders to aim your body properly

My grip, stance, and posture at address are performed out of habit as part of my pre-shot routine. But like a lot of players, I tend to go wrong with my alignment. I'm prone to lining my shoulders too far to the right, causing me to swing outside to in to get the club moving down the target line. My first setup key, then, is to align my feet, hips, and shoulders so they are parallel with the target line. That makes it much easier to return to a sound, powerful position at impact. *Betsy King*

A. Ravielli

12

REACH FOR POWER

Extend your arms out at address to generate more clubhead speed

Women may not be built to hit the ball as far as men, but there are several ways in which we can create more powerful golf swings. To allow the club to gain maximum speed during the downswing and follow-through, reach your arms out at address so your hands are under your nose (top) rather than directly under your shoulders (bottom). This position will assure ultimate extension at impact and in the follow-through, creating power and distance. *Debbie Steinbach*

13

HIT IT LONG

Keep your eyes on the back of the ball for bigger drives

How do you hit the ball farther? That's a question I'm asked all the time by my pro-am partners. I give them this tip, which works like magic: Keep your eyes on the back of the ball from setup through impact and imagine seeing the clubhead hit the ball. This will help your head and upper body stay behind the ball until after the hit, and give you a lot more power. *Nancy Lopez*

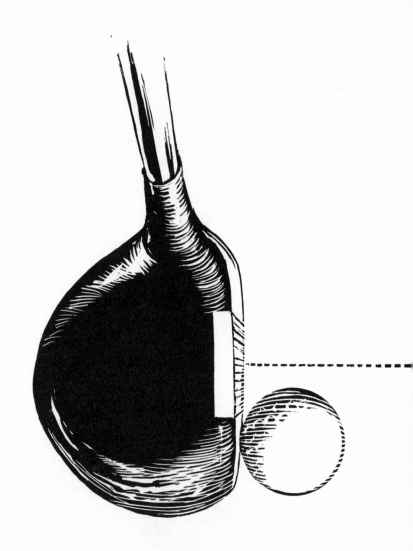

14

CHANGE OF FACE

*Tee the ball nearer the toe
of your driver for more solid
contact*

Do you often hit your tee shots off the heel of your club?
It might be because you're hitting the ball up in the
center of the clubface. For solid contact, the club must
rise to hit the ball at the correct level. When you tee the
ball in the center of the clubface, you'll notice that as
the club rises, contact will occur more toward the heel.
Try teeing the ball nearer to the toe of the club so that
as the club rises through impact it will make contact in
the sweet spot. Watch this small change produce big
results. *Susie Meyers*

15

FOOT MEASUREMENTS

Set your heels about shoulder-width apart for your driver, but no more

Your stance, as a general rule, should never be wider than your shoulders. A stance that is wider than your shoulders will inhibit your ability to make a turn, and it often promotes a hip sway, or lateral slide. When you slide rather than rotate, you create very little resistance between your upper and lower body, which translates into a loss of power. Practice a consistent setup: Your heels should be about hip-width apart for your irons and up to shoulder-width apart for your driver and fairway woods. *Kellie Stenzel*

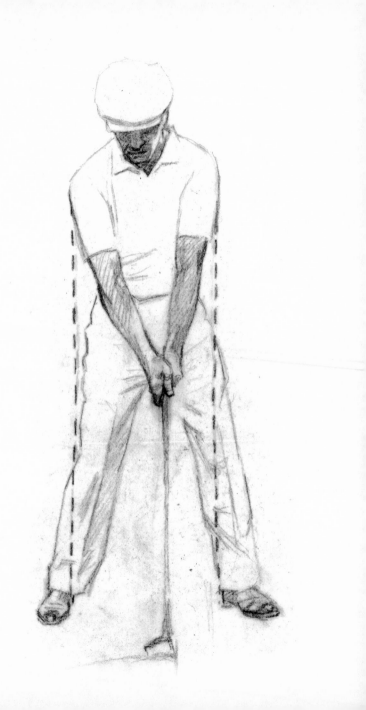

16

CURVES AHEAD

Adjust your setup, not your swing, to fade and draw the ball

To hit a good fade, I make two adjustments to my setup, then make my normal swing. First, I aim as far left of the target as I want the ball start. Second, I open the clubface, pointing it to where I want the ball to land.

To draw the ball, my pre-shot adjustments are the opposite of those I make to hit a fade. First, I aim my body to the right, where I want the ball to start. Second, I close the clubface so it faces where I want the ball to land. I don't change my grip or my swing. And I don't swing any harder or easier. With both of these shots, I trust that the set-up changes I made will produce a different shot when I make my standard golf swing. **Lorena Ochoa**

17

GET SHORTY

Turn your right toe in to deter you from overswinging

Many players believe that in order to hit the ball farther they have to take a bigger backswing. As a result they end up over-rotating—and taking the club back past parallel—which actually robs them of both power and control.

After taking your normal stance, turn your right toe a couple of inches to the left. Your right foot's position will prevent you from turning your hips too much, which in turn will stop your upper body and arms from over-rotating. The resulting shorter back-swing will help you hit the ball straighter and farther.

Kellie Stenzel

18

DISTANCE FROM THE BALL

The length of the shaft determines ball position

As your golf club gets shorter, your shaft angle gets steeper. It's easier to make a descending blow from the steeper plane of a pitching wedge than it is from the flatter plane of a 7-wood.

Ball position is also determined by the length of the shaft. As the shaft gets shorter, your ball position moves closer to the center of your stance. A wedge is normally played from the middle. As the club gets shorter, your stance will narrow and you will stand closer to the ball. *Judy Rankin*

3.Swin

A. Ravielli

g

19

HOLD IT STEADY

Keep your head still through impact to hit the ball solidly

If you keep your concentration on the ball—or, as Harvey Penick says, keep your eye underneath the ball and clip the grass underneath the ball—you're not likely to move your head up and down. Otherwise, you'd lose sight of the ball and the grass, as well as any real chance for a good shot.

Head position is critical. Some golfers confuse moving weight to the left side with moving the head. You don't move your head to the left side; you move your weight. Your head has to stay in place until after impact; then it moves. *Kathy Whitworth*

20

SWING YOUR DRIVER LIKE A 'U'

A sweeping approach will help you gain more distance

Because the ball is on a tee, driver impact should be a sweeping motion. Picture the swing arc as a "U," where the downswing bottoms out gradually, unlike the up-and-down "V" shape of a wedge swing. And swing your driver at the same speed you do every other club. For me, a 6 or 7 out of 10 is the right speed.

Amateurs tend to tee the ball too low and too far back in their stance, and then hit down on it. Tee up so that half the ball is above the clubface, and play the ball off your front instep. From there, you can shift forward on the downswing and extend your arms.

Annika Sorenstam

21

*Stay in your angles through
impact to hit more solid shots*

Many golfers incorrectly rise
up or drop down in their backswing, or stop and rise up
at impact. Successful players move "to" the golf ball
and "through" it. Like them, you want to be firing down
and through the ball. Stay in your posture as you move
though the impact area and you'll make the most of
your iron shots. *Judy Rankin*

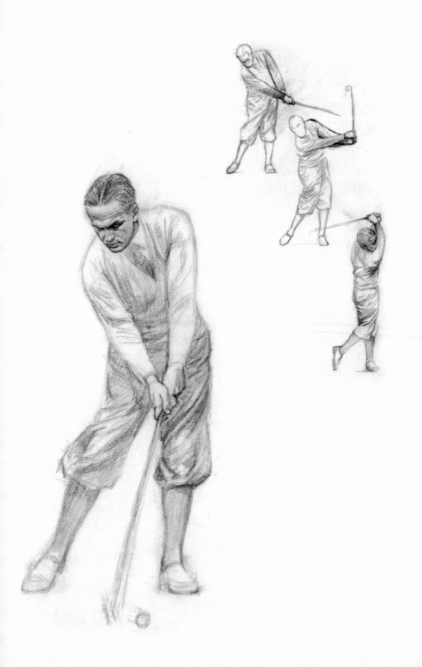

22

JUMPSTART YOUR DOWNSWING

Push off your right leg to apply more force to the ball

I get a lot of power by pushing off on my right leg on the downswing. I can feel the pressure on my right foot digging in, giving me the strength that I want for getting through the shot. At the same time, my left leg is firm as I shift my weight from the right side to the left side. My wrists uncock and sort of snap right through the ball. Hearing that click as the result of good hand and arm action is one of the most beautiful sounds in golf. *Nancy Lopez*

23

IRONS: NO WRIST BREAK

Think low and straight on the takeaway

Swing the clubhead away from the ball low and straight without breaking your wrists on the backswing. As with the woods, the start of the backswing is an all-together rotation of hips and shoulders carrying the arms and hands with it, wrists unbroken, while the clubhead moves straight back from the ball, low to the ground. The tendency of most people, especially with irons, is to pick the clubhead up entirely with the wrists.

Betsy Rawls

24

LASH AT THE BALL

Active hands are the key to more distance

Distance relates largely to the release of the hands and wrists in the impact zone. The faster a golfer can move the clubhead through the ball, the farther she will hit it.

Women who want to add distance should get the feeling that the hit is a left-handed, backhanded lash at the ball. There is no need to be concerned with the right hand, because it will provide its own power naturally.

It has been my experience that a golfer can hit the ball fairly well with this kind of release even if she's swinging relatively flat-footed, with little body pivot. However, even with a good full pivot it isn't possible to really sting the ball unless your hands are "alive." *Louise Suggs*

25

HIT YOUR WOODS FLUSH

Shift your weight to your left side to avoid topping the ball

Hitting fairway and utility woods with authority requires a weight shift to the left side to start the downswing. Many players, however, try to initiate the downswing from the upper part of the body, rather than the lower part. This can lead to hanging back on the right side with no weight shift to the left.

One helpful drill my teacher, Harvey Penick, gave me was to set up aimed at the pitcher's mound and be sure to finish aimed toward the shortstop position left of the mound. What that mental drill does is make you swing the club all the way through and turn your body toward the target. *Kathy Whitworth*

26

ROTATE YOUR CENTER

Increase your distance with the help of your core

Why is it that when I try to take five yards off a shot, I usually wind up hitting the ball farther? It's because my backswing tempo slows down, which allows for a smoother transition and a natural acceleration of the club on the forward swing. When I need to carry a fairway bunker or hit the ball 10 yards farther, I increase the tempo of my forward swing. I do this by rotating the center of my body faster through the shot; I feel as if I'm hitting the ball more with my legs and hips. I'm not trying to swing harder, I'm maximizing the power of my body's rotation. *Lorena Ochoa*

27

LOAD THE RIGHT SIDE

Use this drill to get behind the ball and stop swaying

On the backswing, your weight moves off your left side to the inside of your right foot, leg and knee. Many golfers overdo the weight shift, so that their weight ends up on the outside of their right foot. This swaying action will hamper your ability to get into a nice, tight coil, and you'll lose power.

To learn to make your turn against a firm right side, place the grip end of a club under the outside of your right foot (or use a golf ball) and begin hitting balls with your right foot and knee braced in this position. The object will prevent you from swaying to the outside, and you'll feel resistance, which is created by the shifting of your weight against your right side. Notice how your right knee serves as an anchor around which you make your shoulder turn. *Kathy Whitworth*

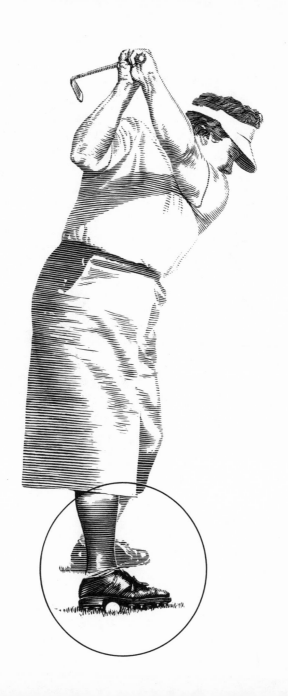

28

STRETCH YOUR LEFT SIDE

A simple image to create a wider arc—and more distance

A wide arc is a "must" for achieving both distance and accuracy in golf shots. The only move I consciously try to make to obtain a wider arc is to have a definite sensation of stretching my left arm and the muscles of my left side on the backswing.

As you stretch, your left shoulder should turn under your chin. If it does not, it is an indication that you are simply lifting the club up rather than swinging it. Stretching produces a straight—though not stiff—left arm. *Mickey Wright*

29

KEEP RIGHT ELBOW CLOSE

How to control the length of your backswing

The position of your right elbow at the top of the swing can affect the length of your backswing. Focus on keeping the elbow close to your body and directly under your hands—much like a waiter holding up a tray. If the elbow flies out, away from your body, the right shoulder comes up with it and the club crosses the line (or points right of the target). Get the elbow to point down, not out, and you'll be in a better position to start your downswing. *Lorena Ochoa*

30

FANCY FOOTWORK

Use your feet to shift your weight properly in the swing

In golf, as in most sports, good balance stems from good footwork. At the address position your weight should be evenly distributed between your two feet and carried on both the ball and heel of each foot. On the backswing your weight should be transferred from *across* your left foot to the *inside* of your right, so that at the top of your backswing most of the weight is on the right. On the downswing the first movement should be to shift this weight back to your left foot.

The transfer of weight in the golf swing is not a big or complete shifting, but merely enough to maintain balance and rhythm as the body turns and the club moves back and then forward. *Mickey Wright*

31

THE FIRST 12 INCHES

'Kill' the hips for a better turn.

To me, the single most important element of the swing is the takeaway, and I've discovered over the years that I get the best results with a move that involves the hands, arms and shoulders simultaneously. The hips are, in a word, dead.

    I try to take my hands at least one foot back before the hips start to turn. If the arm swing is done properly, the hips will follow of their own accord. I don't even think about them. What this takeaway achieves for me is a smoother backswing and a full shoulder turn. *Joanne Carner*

32

PATH AND PLANE

Analyzing the lines of your swing

The "arc" that the club shaft scribes is called the "swing plane." The clubhead itself also makes an arc on its route back and through, referred to as the clubhead path.

The clubshaft needs to form a circular plane, one that leans to the side. The amount of lean varies according to the height and build of a person. The shaft also needs to return to the original shaft plane (an imaginary line drawn through the shaft and the body at address) at impact. Nearly all good players accomplish this, some with many more compensations and manipulations than others. *Patti McGowan*

33

HANDS LEAD THE TAKEAWAY

Move them straight back for a more level backswing turn

A lot of amateurs begin the backswing by dipping the left shoulder and "picking up" the club with the hands. This causes the clubface to close and prevents the shifting of weight needed to store power at the top of the swing. A weak, slice-producing "over-the-top" downswing often results.

My first thought is to move my hands straight back on the takeaway for about a foot. If I can get my hands started in good fashion, a level shoulder turn and a good backswing will follow naturally.

Liselotte Neumann

34

USE YOUR HEAD

Allow your head to turn toward the target for crisper contact

Shots from the fairway should not be thought of as power shots. Don't swing your hands back to 12 o'clock, as you might with a driver. Stop at 10 o'clock, and fight the tendency to hang back on your right side and scoop the ball off the ground. Hit down on it by making a good shift to your left side.

When I was a kid, my coach Henri Reis had me hit balls turning my head toward the target before impact to create more forward rotation. I worked on this so much, it became part of my swing. I'm glad I did, because it helps me get to my front side and make a downward strike. *Annika Sorenstam*

35

EASY DOES IT

*Develop clubhead speed slowly
to deliver maximum power*

A good swing rhythm is vital in
allowing the clubhead to reach maximum speed in the
hitting area. I have found that the best way to develop
good rhythm is to instill a clear mental picture of a
swing in your mind before ever stepping up to the ball.
In your swing you merely develop the picture, then
transfer it into your own movement.

I usually picture one of three things:

- A child's playswing moving back and forth.
- A pitcher delivering a softball.
- A fine golfer's swing, such as Sam Snead's or
  Louise Suggs's.

From each of these mental pictures I derive a slow,
graceful buildup of power and clubhead speed. There
should be no single point of sudden acceleration.

Mickey Wright

36

NO SLOWING DOWN

Wrap the club around your shoulders into one big follow-through

My follow-through is a big, sweeping extension of the swing. I just let everything go, as though I couldn't stop the swing if I wanted to. The club is wrapped around my shoulders, and my entire body is facing the target. I notice so often in watching women amateurs that they quit on the swing right after impact. How much more effective it is to sweep the club through with a full extension! *Nancy Lopez*

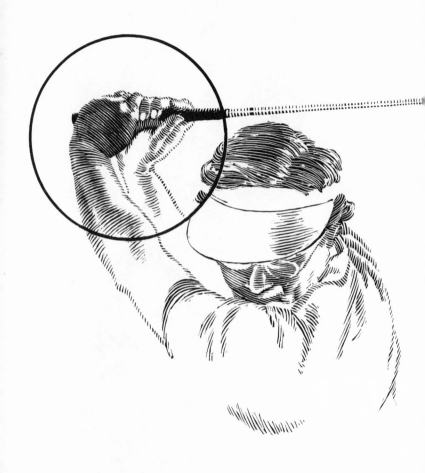

WRISTY BUSINESS

Gain more distance by hinging your wrists properly in the backswing

Hand-wrist action constitutes the most important factor in a golf swing. This is especially true for women golfers who might not have the advantage of strong shoulder, trunk, and leg muscles. They must utilize every bit of power available in their wrists and hands.

The wrists don't start to cock until they reach about waist height. At the top of the backswing, I want the toe of the clubhead pointing at the ground, and I want my wrists fully cocked and under the shaft. Properly and fully cocked, the wrists are thus in a position to remain cocked until near impact on the downswing, and thus apply the power of which they are capable. *Patty Berg*

38

RIGHT KNEE FLEX

Maintain a slight bend to your right leg in the backswing

Keeping the legs too straight is an error infrequently detected in women players because it is hidden by skirts. If the legs are straight it becomes almost impossible to create the proper hip and body action. Improper body action can result in a variety of errors—topping and slicing particularly.

My feeling is that the turn of the body (pivot) is created by the legs. When the knees are stiff, the legs can't work properly. Check to ascertain whether your right knee remains bent and braced, with your weight on the inside of your right foot, on the backswing. *Betsy Rawls*

A. Ravielli

39

FINISH WHAT YOU STARTED

Maximize clubhead speed by learning the correct follow-through

Just because the ball's gone doesn't mean the swing's over. Every swing has a start and a finish, and you'll maximize your speed only if you don't interrupt that chain reaction. At the end, you want to be balanced with your right foot vertical and your right knee, right hip, and right shoulder in line with a straight left leg. Your legs should be close enough to hold a towel between your knees. *Gale Peterson*

PATIENCE IS KEY

Allow the club to come to a slow pause at the top of your back swing

40

One thing my coach has always preached to me is patience during the transition from back to forward swing. Often, he'll say the word to me just before I start bringing the club back, or sometimes at the top of my swing, just to test my concentration. When I'm patient, my back swing comes to a very slow pause at the top. There's no rushing the club down, which gives me time to initiate the downswing with my lower body and shift my weight forward, onto my front side.

My transition feels like one long, slow movement. It's not broken up into parts—slow and fast, or fast and faster. The club starts down at the same speed at which it finishes. *Lorena Ochoa*

41

SWING ACROSS YOUR LAP

Brush your right hip to promote a powerful release

Think of keeping your elbows together throughout your swing, and almost brush your right hip with your right elbow as you swing through the impact area. This puts the club on the proper track—from inside to along the target line—and sets up the proper sequence of motion that produces clubhead speed and, subsequently, power.

Peggy Kirk Bell

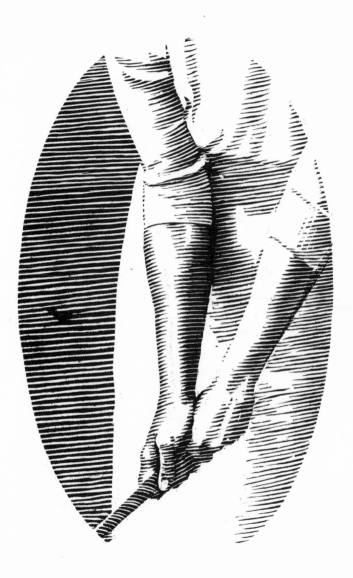

42

MOMENTUM CHANGER

Practice with a headcover on your driver to build more clubhead speed

Picture a child's swing set. The swing travels back, then stops momentarily at the top before it changes direction and starts down, picking up momentum and speed along the way. It makes one flowing motion, not a series of jerky starts and stops. The golf swing should work in a similar fashion, the clubhead accelerating through impact to a complete finish with no interruptions, pauses or stops.

To learn how to accelerate the club through impact into a full, balanced finish, practice swinging with your headcover on your driver. The additional resistance on the clubhead will force you to drive it through impact into a full finish, and will teach you how to use tempo to generate more clubhead speed and power.

Karen Palacios-Jansen

A. Ravielli

43

HOLD YOUR FINISH

Stay in balance to keep your tempo in check

Tempo is the first thing to go when you try to overpower the ball. Even the thought of more power can create tension, and tense muscles don't move smoothly. To stay relaxed, start at address: Keep your grip light and your wrists and arms soft.

One way to tell if your tempo is too fast is to try to hold your finish. If you have trouble keeping your balance, it's time to tone down your speed. In practice sessions I'll even raise my right foot to make sure I'm balanced over my left side. Use this as a drill or practice swing when your tempo feels out of control.

Annika Sorenstam

44

HOGAN'S FUNDAMENTALS

While his swing was a thing of beauty, it was his precision and focus that influenced me most as a young girl

My father, Paul Torluemke, was a big fan of Ben Hogan. I don't know if he ever saw Hogan play in person, but he was a great admirer of his ability to focus. While some would call Hogan stoic and unable to smile, my father saw in him an innate ability to concentrate,

and he wanted me to do that, too. My father loved the precision part of his game, because he was so dogged on hitting fairways and greens. That was the kind of player I was raised to be. I guess some of it took, because I hit a lot of fairways and greens during the best years of my LPGA career.

Still pictures were all we had back in the early 1950s, and while my swing evolved mainly from trial and error, many swings in that era were patterned after Hogan's. And for good reason: There's much to be learned from Hogan's swing, for both men *and* women. Turn the page for my swing analysis. *Judy Rankin*

45

EARLY EXTENSION

A wide arc is essential to building more clubhead speed

There's a comfortable extension of the arms and club during the early part of Hogan's swing, producing a very wide swing arc. Many women, in an effort to create width, move with the club and sway off the ball. But Hogan's weight remains inside his feet and there is no visible sign of tension in his arms. This is textbook.

A wide swing arc helps you generate more clubhead speed and power. To get it, think of the club as an extension of your left arm, from your shoulder down to the clubhead, and keep this straight line intact during the first few feet of your backswing. Extend your arms as comfortably as you can without allowing your weight to drift outside your right hip. *Judy Rankin*

46

WRIST COCK

*Use your wrists as hinges,
not your elbows*

As Hogan's hands reach waist-height, the club is almost set. The clubshaft and Hogan's left arm form close to a 90-degree angle, creating leverage which he will unleash on the downswing for a more powerful burst of speed through the ball.

Many women use their elbows as a hinge instead of their wrists, often due to a lack of strength in their wrists and forearms. This significantly collapses and narrows the swing's arc. Hinge the club up at your wrists, just above your left thumb joint, so that your hands are in position to support the club. At the top of the swing, your hands should be underneath the grip and the club should feel very light, not heavy. If it feels light, then you're in a good position to start your downswing. *Judy Rankin*

BACKSWING COIL

Resist with your lower body to create a tighter, more powerful wind-up

One thing I see in this frame and throughout Hogan's backswing is that his feet and hips are very quiet. There's a subtle shift of weight to his right side and his shoulders are rotating, but there is no lateral sway off the ball.

As a general rule, women tend to be more full-body turners than men. Their feet, legs, and hips are very active in the backswing, whereas men do a much better job of restricting their hip turn and coiling against the resistance of their lower body. This resistance creates a stronger backswing coil and a lot more power.

Picture a rubber band dangling from your right hand. If you twist the bottom end in both directions, nothing happens. But if you hold the bottom end still and turn the top, you create more stretch and energy in the elastic band. You want to recreate the same feeling of resistance in your backswing, which you can do by keeping your feet grounded and your lower body quiet.

And remember, it is not wrong to lift your left heel off the ground if it's necessary to complete your backswing turn. *Judy Rankin*

48

STEADY ON THE RIGHT

Keep the right knee slightly bent to load up properly on the backswing

Hogan makes a nice, full shoulder turn, rotating his left shoulder under his chin. But what is most significant about this frame is how his right knee remains slightly flexed and virtually unchanged from its address position—other than that it is turned in ever so slightly. The knee remains stable throughout the backswing, which allows him to load up on his right side so his weight can naturally shift forward, toward the target, on the downswing.

If you allow the right knee to straighten, your upper body tilts toward the target at the top of the backswing—what is commonly known as a reverse pivot. From this position, your weight has no place to go but backwards. Focus on keeping your right knee slightly bent on the backswing. You should feel your weight settling on your right heel as you reach the top.

Judy Rankin

49

STAY WITH IT

Maintain your posture through impact for solid contact

After impact, Hogan's right heel is just starting to come off the ground. He is beginning to release his head to follow the flight of the ball and has yet to come out of his posture—further evidence of his great body control. This is important. In order to hit the ball solidly, you must maintain your posture—or the angles established by your body at address—throughout the shot. Many women come up out of their posture early by lifting their head and spine up, which usually results in a topped or thin shot.

Hogan's weight has already shifted to his left leg and his hips have begun to turn—or clear—out of the way so his arms can swing through freely. His head and upper body are ever so slightly behind the ball, which is a key to hitting the ball straight.

Judy Rankin

50

CLIP THE GRASS

Be careful not to hit down on the ball too much

Tell a conscientious golf student to hit down on the ball, and the first move in the downswing is likely to be a big shift to the left accompanied by a premature shoulder rotation. It creates a wood-chopping sort of stroke.

Instead of swinging an axe, a player would be better to swing a weed cutter. If you hit the ball at the lowest point in your swing, as though you are clipping the grass with a weed cutter, that's hitting down enough.

Harvey Penick with Betty Hicks

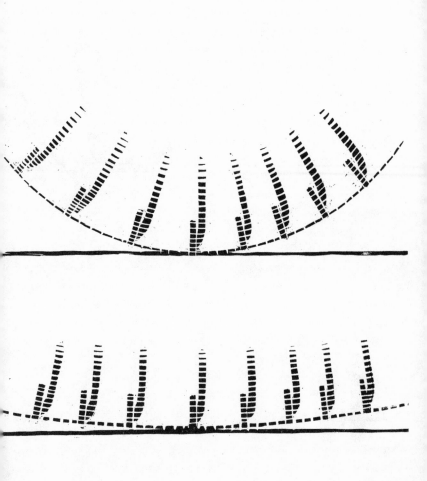

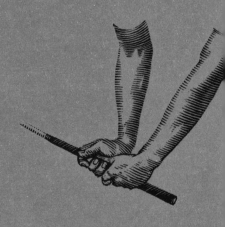

4.Chip

ping

51

PRECISE PITCHING

Abbreviate your finish for more control on short shots

Pitching is about accuracy and distance control, so your finish should be shorter and more compact than it would be with your driver or irons. Keep the length of your backswing and forward swing equal—roughly waist-high to waist-high for a pitch of thirty yards. A more abbreviated finish means less excess motion in the swing, making it easier to hit the ball solidly.

Finish with your arms extended in front of your body. By coming to a controlled stop, you avoid the common mistake of decelerating the clubhead through impact, which leads to poor contact. *Cristie Kerr*

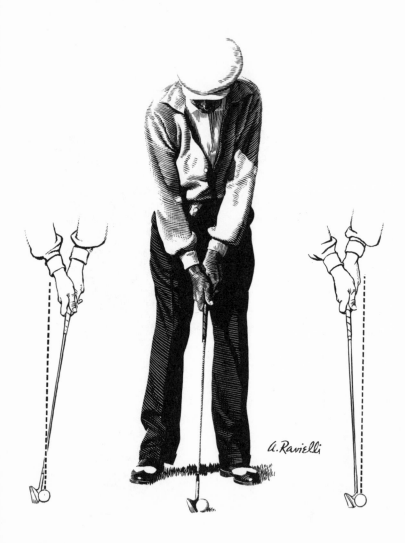

52

SHORT-GAME SHOTMAKING

Adjust your ball position to hit high, soft pitches and low, bump-and-run shots

Many people don't realize it, but the key to executing different types of shots is ball position. For the high-lofted shot, I set up so the ball is more centered in my stance. This way, the club (a sand wedge) will slide under the ball and allow me to toss it high into the air and land it softly on the green. For the bump-and-run shot, I use a 7-iron and move the ball slightly back in my stance. With the ball back, I automatically hit it with my hands farther ahead of the clubhead, delofting the club (in other words, making it act more like a 5-iron), which makes the ball fly lower, land harder, and run up to the hole. *Judy Rankin*

53

PRACTICE WITH PURPOSE

Simulate real playing conditions as much as possible

Spend at least half your practice time simulating playing conditions. Change lies, clubs, targets, and distances; don't go on to the next shot until you get it right. If you're practicing around the green, use one ball and play it until you hole out with your putter. Go through your normal routines before each shot as if you were playing for real. If you want to play better golf, you need to practice better golf. *Lynn Marriott and Pia Nilsson*

A. Ravielli

A. Ravielli

54

TELLING TIME

Use the image of a clockface to better gauge the length of your swing

For greater precision on 30- to 60-yard pitch shots, use clockface positions to determine swing length. Start with a backswing length of 9 o'clock and finish at 3 o'clock. Note your average yardage. If you need a little more distance, swing from 10 to 2. A little less distance, swing from 8 to 4. On all shots, swing the club through the ball with good acceleration.

Cathy MacPherson

55

HOW TO ADD LOFT

Open the clubface to create
more height on pitch shots

On a pitch, open the clubface
as you go back (top). This means that the clubface will
be at right angles to the ground at the end of the backswing. If the clubface is square on a pitch as on a
chip, you will defeat the entire purpose of the pitch,
which is to give the ball loft and backspin (bottom).
The process of opening the clubface will cause more
wrist action on a pitch, too. Hit firmly through on the
downswing. *Betsy Rawls*

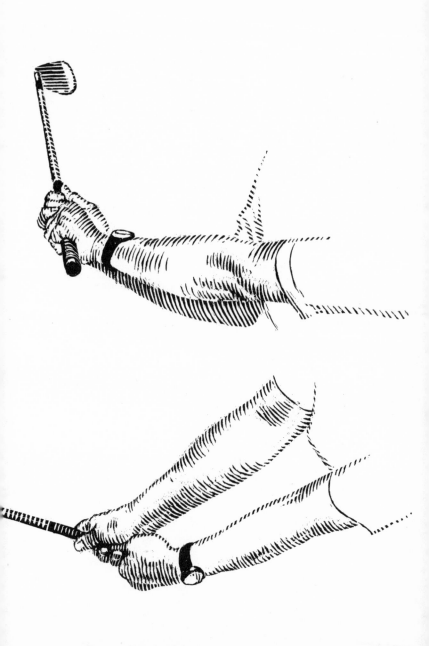

56

A BIG FLOP

Use an underhand motion to loft the ball high and over trouble

Open the clubface and relax your grip. Angle your upper body so your right shoulder is lower than your left. Swing back, set your hands, and swing through without letting your right hand roll over. Pretend that you're throwing a ball underhand with your right hand through the shot. **Heather Daly-Donofrio**

57

CHIP LIKE YOU PUTT

Keep the ball rolling as much as possible for more one-putt greens

There is no question in my mind that women golfers must resort to the chip shot more frequently than do men. It's simple: We don't hit the ball as far as men do. An accurate chip shot that results in a one-putt green is the key to lower scoring.

My chipping style is designed to produce low shots that land close to the near edge of the green and roll as far as possible. I treat these chip shots much like long putts. In deciding how hard I want to hit the ball, I think about how much force I would need to putt the ball that far. The closer I am to the edge of the green, the less lofted club I will use. Under normal circumstances, I'll use a 4-iron from just off the edge, then gradually use more loft until I hit an 8-iron from my extreme chipping range of about 20 feet out.

Sandra Haynie

58

THE LOW-RUNNING CHIP

Maintain a small letter 'y' to hit the ball crisply

To be more consistent around the greens, hit a low, running shot whenever you can. Using a short iron, play the ball just inside your back heel, set your weight left, and push your hands ahead of the ball. Your arms and club should form a lower-case "y" at address.

With the correct setup, the swing is a matter of rocking your shoulders back and through—much like a long putting stroke. Lean into your front side to start the downswing. You want to return to the ball with your "y" perfectly intact. The angles you created at address will produce a downward strike and a low runner that rolls like a putt. *Annika Sorenstam*

59

HIT DOWN AND THROUGH

Groove your 50-yard pitch shot with left-arm only swings

A 50-yard pitch is a must-have shot to score on-par 5s and long-par 4s. Try this drill: With a pitching wedge, set up with the ball in the center of your stance. Swing the club back with an early wrist cock, then swing through to your finish, releasing your right hand from the club at impact. This helps you hit down and through on short pitches—the key to good contact. You can increase distance by swinging your hands higher on the backswing. *Suzy Whaley*

A. Ravielli

60

ROUGH FINESSE

Hit down on the ball sharply to avoid fat contact

When your ball lodges in thick rough near the green, employ a steeper-than-normal attack angle with your pitching wedge to minimize the amount of grass between the clubface and the ball. You will feel as though you are breaking your wrists immediately away from the ball. The follow-through should be the same length as the backswing.

A practice swing is vital. Select a position near your ball where the grass is similar in length and texture to that of your lie. Take a practice swing to evaluate how much resistance the grass will offer.

Betty Hicks

61

BARE ESSENTIALS

Don't swing too hard when hitting off hardpan or other tight surfaces

Oftentimes when your lie is bare, if you don't catch the ball first, you can mis-hit it very easily. Also, if you're standing on a bare spot, don't swing too hard, because you don't want to lose your balance. Take a little extra club so you don't have to swing hard. Keep your head steady—not down, but steady—because if you move up and down during the swing, that's going to cause a mis-hit. *Betsy King*

62

BALL-TURF CONTACT

*Hit down on the ball to strike
your wedges solidly*

In a good wedge swing, the
clubhead hits the ball first and then the ground, leaving
a divot on the target side of the ball. If you tend to hit
your wedges low, with no divot, it's because the clubhead is bottoming out, or reaching its low point, behind
the ball.

Try this drill: Place a pencil three or four inches
behind the ball. Start with a half swing and hit down on
the ball, avoiding the pencil. To hit the ball and not the
pencil, you must shift your weight forward at the start of
the downswing. This brings the bottom of your swing arc
forward, in front of the pencil, so you can hit the ball,
then the turf. *Annika Sorenstam*

63

SHORT PITCH FROM ROUGH

Blast out as if you were hitting a sand shot

Fluffy grass tends to grab the hosel of the club and close the clubface through impact. The sand wedge, because it has more loft and is the heaviest club in the bag, resists that tendency.

Set up as you would for a sand shot: the ball forward in your stance with the clubface open to the 1 o'clock position and the stance open approximately 15 degrees. On the downswing, make the club travel along your stance line. Expect the ball to pop out with less spin and a little more run. *Sandy LaBauve*

5.Putti

ng

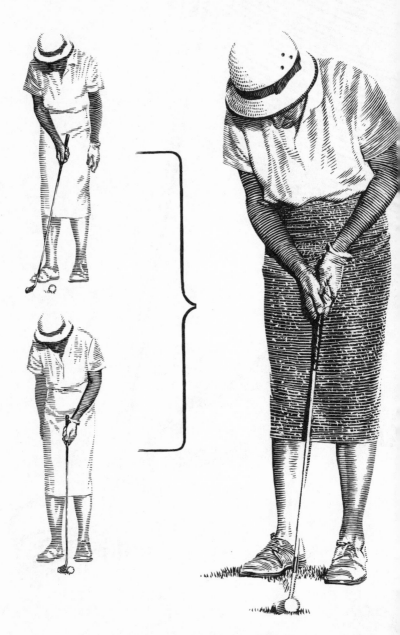

64

WORKING HANDS

How you grip the putter determines how you stroke the ball

Each hand has its own function, but they must work together to swing the club on a steady, consistent path.

I like to think of my right hand as my distance hand, because it dictates how far back and through I take the putter. I point my right finger down the side of the grip to keep the clubhead steady. My left hand is my alignment hand. The back of the hand faces the target, and it keeps the putter square throughout the stroke. *Nancy Lopez*

65

LAY IT FLAT

*Sole the putterhead at address
for a smoother roll*

When my putting goes awry,
it is often because I've allowed my hands to get in too
close to my body at address. When that happens, I get
the toe of the putter off the ground and start to push
and pull putts off line. I have to remember to keep my
hands away from my body a little bit so the putter
sits flat.

When the putter is properly soled, I have a
much better chance of rolling the ball into the cup.
Getting the ball to roll consistently and smoothly
is what I work on. *Patty Sheehan*

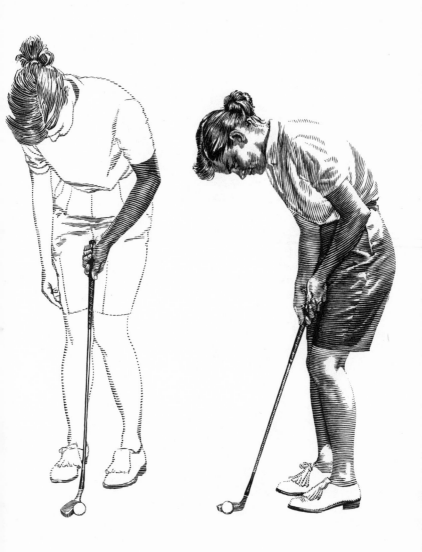

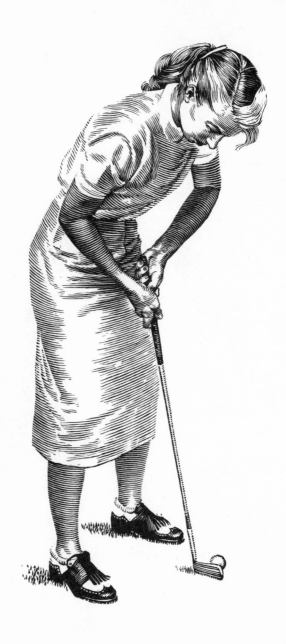

66

LEAD WITH THE LEFT ARM

Keep it moving toward the target to hole more putts

A tip Ken Venturi gave on a television show helped me a lot. He said, "Keep the butt end of the putter moving toward the hole as you stroke through the ball." That's been very successful for me, because it helps me keep my left elbow away from my body. This is important, since the left arm acts as a leader in keeping the club on line. *Patty Sheehan*

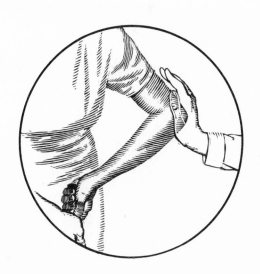

67

PUTT TO THE BREAK

Focus more on the line and less on the hole

      As you read a putt, determine a spot between the ball and the hole where you see the putt beginning to break, or fall, toward the hole. Putt the ball over the spot, keeping speed in mind (the quicker the putt, the more it's going to break). By focusing on the line you intend to stroke the putt on, and not the hole, you're more likely to hit the putt with the correct amount of break and speed. Golfers who aim for the hole generally wind up missing on the low side because they don't account for enough break.

Cristie Kerr

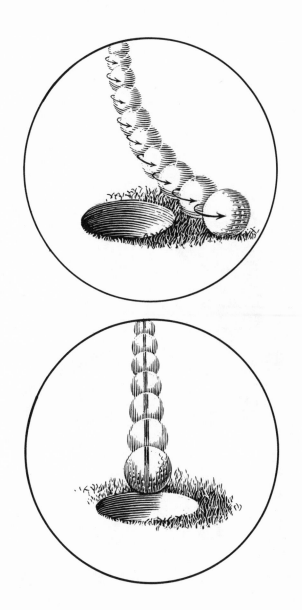

68

Keep your hands in a comfortable, neutral position during the stroke

When putting, your hands should be placed comfortably on the club. Don't grip the putter too tightly because that creates tension in your hands, wrists and forearms. Nothing wrecks a smooth putting stroke faster than tension.

The key to success with any putting grip is keeping your hands in a neutral position—neither too strong or too weak—with your palms facing each other and square to the target. Neutral hands eliminate any rotation (or twisting) of the putterhead during the stroke. One technique I've found useful is holding the putter in the center of my left palm. This produces the feeling of having more control with the blade. **Kathy Whitworth**

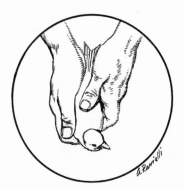

69

UPS AND DOWNS

How to determine the amount of speed and break on hilly putts

Uphill putts require more speed, which reduces the break at the beginning of the putt. Downhill putts move faster, which increases the break. Faster putts break more; slower putts break less.

It's always better to overestimate the break of a putt. The ball will never go in if you start it on a line that's lower than the correct line. However, if you start the putt higher, you can still hole it with the right speed. *Carol Preisinger*

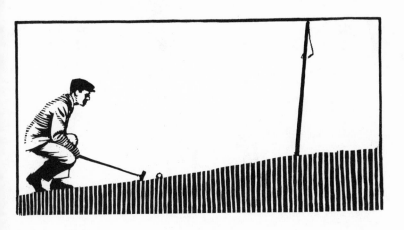

Golf Digest
P.O. Box 37766
Boone, IA 50036-0766

Included with your purchase of *100 Classic Golf Tips from Leading Ladies' Teaching and Touring Pros* is a one-year (12 issues) subscription to either *Golf Digest* or *Golf for Women*, the #1 golf publications. To start receiving your subscription please fill out this original card (no photocopies) and drop in the mail. Please allow 6–8 weeks for delivery of first issue. Offer is open to US residents only.

Golf Digest ☐   *Golf for Women* ☐

Name ....

Address...

....

City...

State..

Zip..

Email ....

70

POP STROKE

Try this method to avoid swaying on putts

The stroke I use is a hand-and-wrist motion with little or no arm movement. I rest my right elbow on my hip for steadiness. This keeps me from swaying and also keeps my head over the ball.

In hitting, I sort of pop the ball and use the same amount of backswing on all lengths of putts except the very short ones. The feel or amount of effort used for the hit thus all comes from the hands and wrists. *Louise Suggs*

71

BACK TO SQUARE

Here's how to get your putts started online

Players often miss putts because they push the ball to the right or pull it to the left. To get your putt started on line, you need to make sure your putterface is square at impact.

As a drill, set up with two balls in front of your putter—one on the toe and one on the heel. Choose a spot on the green as a target for alignment. Make a stroke as if you were hitting a three-foot putt. If the putter hits both balls at the same time and they travel the same distance, your putterface is square. If the balls leave the putter unevenly, you're opening or closing the face during your stroke. *Janet Coles*

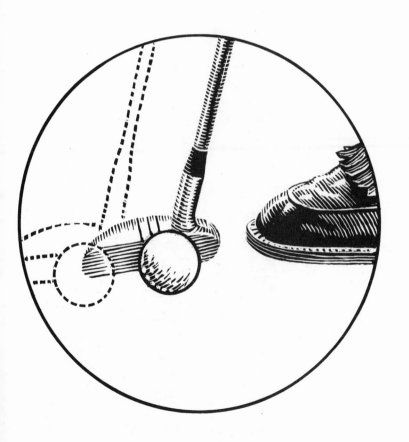

72

EYES OVER THE BALL

A simple method to get you standing the correct distance from the ball

Your eyes must be directly over the ball to enable you to see the proper line to the target. If your eyes aren't directly over the ball, you get a distorted view of the line. If you stand too far from the ball, you'll look inside the line, and you'll probably push most of your putts. If you stand too close to the ball, you'll be looking outside the line, and you'll pull most of your putts.

So keep your head in good position at all times. You might want to visualize the ball at the end of a piece of string that's hanging down from your eyes.

Kathy Whitworth

73

*Keep the putterhead swinging
low past impact*

I notice that when people
struggle with putting, their whole body moves during
the stroke. It's important to stay still over the ball.
I also work on keeping the putter low to the ground
past the impact point by imagining a second ball about
two inches in front of the first. Trying to hit that
second ball keeps my putter low and my body still.

Nancy Lopez

74

PAINT A POSITIVE PICTURE

Let your subconscious guide your putting stroke

The really important thing in putting is holding a positive picture in your mind's eye of the ball rolling toward the cup and dropping into the hole. When you hold such a "picture" in your mind, your subconscious will direct your muscles to move the putter n such a way as to "develop" the picture you are holding. Your putter will then send the ball at a certain speed and in a certain direction that will give it the best possible chance to drop.

If you think of three or four things while stroking the putt, you will find it impossible to hold this mental picture. Once you have "read" the green to the best of your ability, lined the putter blade up at a right angle to the direction you want your ball to start, and visualized a positive picture, then I think the only thing you should concentrate on is contacting the ball as solidly as possible. *Mickey Wright*

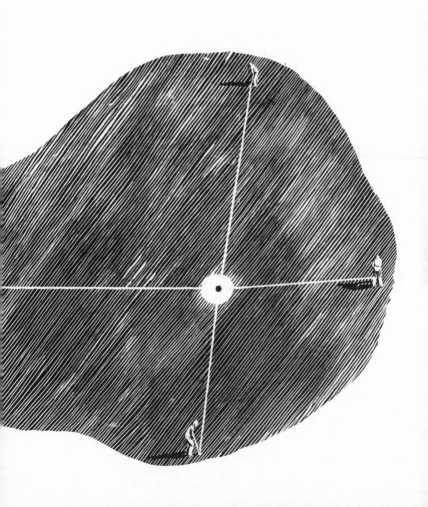

75

AT CLOSE RANGE

Control the stroke with your shoulders to make more short putts… and no peeking!

Being a good putter from short range is all about the putterface. Set it square at address, and keep it that way by controlling the stroke with your shoulders, not your hands. Rock your hands back and through, with the butt of the club staying pointed at your midsection.

On short putts in competition, I focus on my routine. I step in with my right foot first, set the putterface at a right angle to the line, and then complete my stance. From there, I make a shoulder-driven stroke, keeping my eyes down—even the slightest peek can throw the putt off line. *Annika Sorenstam*

6.Sand

Shots

76

HIT ONE INCH BEHIND THE BALL

*Contact the sand first,
then the ball*

The reason they call it an "explosion" shot is because
you hit the sand first, then the ball. The ball rides out
on the cushion of sand that was "exploded" by your
sand wedge.

The question is always how far behind the
ball you should hit, since we've all heard that advice.
Some people say an inch or inch and a half. The best
way is to determine where you think the bottom of
your swing arc will fall, then place the ball an inch
forward of that. The bottom of the arc will usually be
in about the center of your stance with a short iron.
So if you play the ball ahead of that, you will hit
behind it. That's a lot better than trying to play the
ball back and then hit an inch behind it—that's
when you dig in. *Kathy Whitworth*

77 EGG BEATER

*Hit the back edge of the crater
to crack a fried-egg lie*

Play this like a normal bunker shot, but with a square—rather than open—clubface. This will allow the clubhead to get underneath the ball, which is sitting in its own crater of sand. Try to hit the sand at the back edge of the crater and take a bigger divot than normal. Speed is critical, so make sure to accelerate the clubhead through the sand into a full finish. *Carol Preisinger*

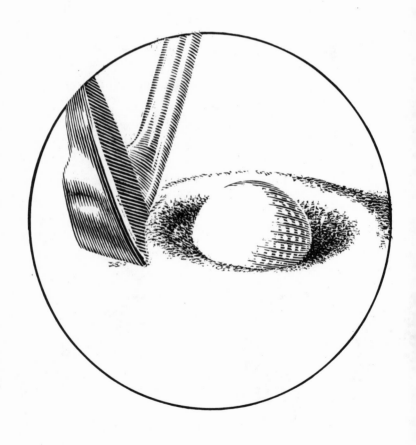

78

BURIED LIE

'Chop out' the ball to escape the bunker in one shot

Occasionally your ball will bury in the sand. This is especially true if you are playing a course that has very fine, soft sand.

First, close the clubface, because this is a shot where the club must dig down into the sand, not glide through it. Next, because you want to hit this shot with a sharply descending blow, play the ball back in your stance, opposite your right foot. You want to take the club away from the ball on a steep angle, quickly cocking your wrists. Drive the clubhead down sharply behind the ball, "chopping down" into the sand and through the hitting area. Unlike a regular bunker shot, where you want to take a thin slice of sand from under the ball, in this shot you must dig down sharply to get the ball up and out. *Amy Alcott*

79

REMOVE THE PILLOW

Try this simple practice tip to blast your way out of the sand

Many beginners have problems with bunkers—getting out of them, that is. When you practice bunker shots, imagine your ball sitting on a little pillow. You can even draw a little pillow in the sand surrounding your ball. You have to hit the pillow and take the ball with it. This helps you get a feeling of how much sand to take. *Helen Alfredsson*

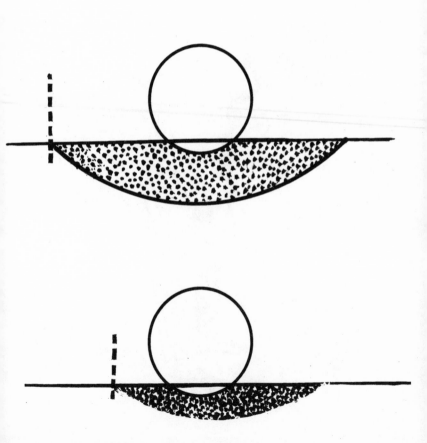

80

HIGH LIP BUNKERS

*Open the clubface and swing
hard to get the ball up quickly*

To hit a short bunker shot over a
high lip, you have to keep the clubface open. That starts
at address: Holding the club with your right hand, rotate
the face 30 degrees open, then set your left hand and
reposition your right. Take a wide stance for stability—
you'll be making a firm swing—and play the ball just
inside your left heel.

Swing the clubhead into the sand about an inch
behind the ball. With the clubface open, you'll have to
swing pretty hard to push the ball up and out. Keep your
wrists firm as you splash through the sand, with the face
pointing straight up. Turn your shoulders through so they
face the target at the finish. *Annika Sorenstam*

81

IRONS: HIT DOWN AND THROUGH

Use the club's loft to elevate the ball for you

People don't realize that the iron swing, particularly on the long ones, is almost exactly the same as with the woods. The only difference is that because you play the ball farther back from your left foot (that is more toward the center of your stance), you hit the ball slightly on the downswing, instead of slightly on the upswing as with a driver off the tee. Too many people try to pick an iron shot clean, or lift it. You must hit down and through the ball with your irons, allowing the natural, built-in loft of the club to elevate the shot for you. Given a chance with the correct swing, it will. *Betsy Rawls*

82

MAKE A SPLASH

Learn how to throw the sand onto the green

Because the clubface doesn't contact the ball (the ball rides out on a cushion of sand), the key to success is to splash, or displace, sand. To get comfortable with this sensation, get in the bunker (no ball) and swing away. Splash the sand as far out of the bunker as you can. Feel the club being grabbed by the sand. Keep the club moving to a full finish. You can have the biggest, baddest, meanest backswing, but if you don't follow through, the ball isn't going anywhere.

Jane Frost

83

LONG AND SMOOTH

Make an even-tempoed three-quarter swing from the sand

For some players, taking a shot out of the sand may seem about as much fun as getting a shot from the doctor. But it needn't be such a terrible experience. The secret to getting the ball out of the bunker from a reasonably good lie is good tempo. Keying on tempo encourages you to make a fuller, more fluid swing. In golf, "tempo" refers to maintaining consistent swing pace or speed, not necessarily being deliberate or slow. So rather than making a short, violent dig into the sand that words such as "blast" bring to mind, try a longer, smoother stroke. (Most good bunker players on the LPGA Tour take a three-quarter swing.). This will allow the clubhead to enter the sand behind the ball and travel through the sand under the ball. *Judy Rankin*

84

BUNKER SETUP

Lay the clubace open to hit the ball high and soft

Be sure to open the face of your sand wedge before you hit a bunker shot. It's helpful to imagine balancing a quarter on the face of the club as you set up for the shot. If the coin would slide off, you don't have the face open enough. The sand wedge is designed to plow through the sand, but only if you get in this open position.

As with the lob, you swing along the line in front of your feet, which causes you to cut across the ball to send the ball toward the target. *Jane Crafter*

A. Ravielli

85

*Dig in and 'splash' out from
a greenside bunker*

"Splash" is the key word here.
You want to splash the sand out onto the green and let
the ball ride the wave of sand out. Here's how:

1) Dig your feet in so the sand is covering the
soles of your shoes, which will improve your balance.
2) Open the clubface to expose the bounce and add loft
to the shot. 3) Place the ball just forward of center in
your stance and brace your weight on your left side to
keep your entry point in the sand more consistent.
4) Hold the clubface open and swing your right arm
down, out and forward. Your hands and arms should
remain soft to ensure smooth acceleration, a full finish
and a clean escape every time. **Gale Peterson**

86

MAKE A CLEAN ESCAPE

How to hit the ball solid from fairway bunkers

The secret to hitting the ball flush is keeping your lower body quiet so you don't lose your footing. To do this, I pinch in my knees at address. As you swing back, keep your weight centered, and then shift smoothly into your downswing. Hit the ball first, then the sand.

Don't quit on the shot, as many amateurs do. Turn through to your left side, and swing your hands up over your left shoulder. You want your right foot up on its toe at the finish and your belt buckle facing the target. *Annika Sorenstam*

87

SAND SOLUTIONS

*Keep your weight left and throw
the club for a clean escape*

Keep your weight on your left
side. From there, it should be easier to hinge the club
upward in the backswing. Coming down, you want to
use the bounce of the club and feel almost like you're
throwing the club from the top. Listen for a smack or
similar sound as the club hits the sand. *Cristie Kerr*

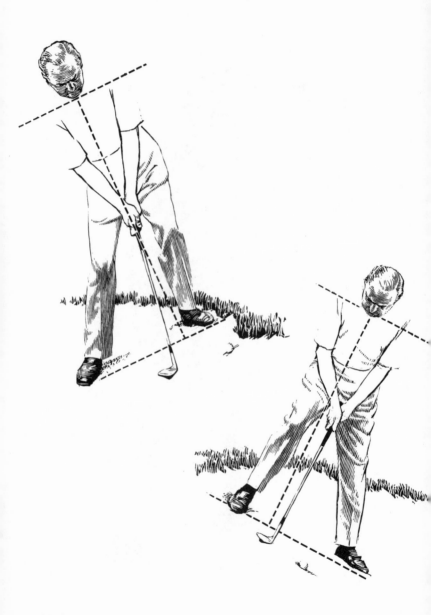

88

UNEVEN LIES

Swing with the slope on uphill and downhill lies

When hitting from an uphill or downhill lie, set your body (knees, hips, shoulders) parallel to the slope, and swing with the slope. From a downhill lie, play the ball just back of center—on the high part of the slope—and hinge the club up sharply going back. Set your weight forward, on your left foot, and keep it there throughout the entire shot.

Carol Preisinger

7.Othe

89

LAY UP SAFELY

Make sure to play short of any hazards

Club selection is key when laying up—sometimes even a wedge or a 9-iron will suffice. Whatever you do, don't over-club. A 7- or 9-wood may work well from the rough, but if you can reach the hazard with either, leave it in the bag. As my dad always told me, if you're going to lay up, lay up short. You don't want to get into more trouble than you're already in. *Nancy Lopez*

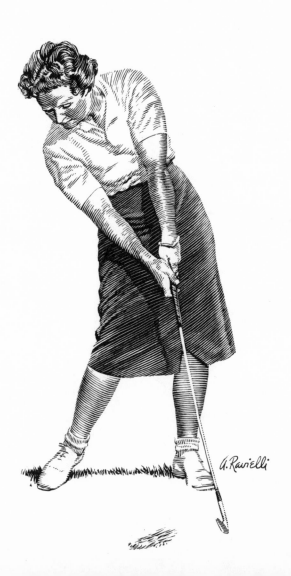

90

BETTER BALL-STRIKING

Imagine you're sweeping the clubhead through the ball

In order to make good contact with the ball, you need to sweep the clubhead through it and toward the target, with an even, confident tempo. Imagine you're using a broom to sweep dirt off a sidewalk. Practice taking the club back low and slow with a good shoulder turn, and then turn through impact, just letting the ball get in the way of your clubface. *Andree Martin*

91

START YOUR SWING EARLY

For a smooth takeaway, imagine the clubhead starting in front of the ball

For your swing to start off smoothly, your body can't be too rigid; you need to feel loose and relaxed over the ball. To promote a smooth takeaway, practice a few swings starting with the club a foot or so in front of the ball. Notice how the club flows back in one easy motion. Now, swing the clubhead back from its normal position behind the ball, maintaining the feel of that same free-flowing motion. *Lynn Marriott and Pia Nilsson*

92

PLAYING FROM A DOWNHILL LIE

Stay down through impact to get the ball airborne

If you're going for it from a downhill lie, you'll need to make these adjustments in your swing: Set your feet and hips parallel to the slope. Move the ball slightly back in your stance. Swing along the slope, or you'll hit it fat. It's also easy to come out of your posture because the ball is below you. Try to maintain your balance through the swing. Abbreviate your follow-through if that helps you stay down through impact. **Wendy Ward**

A. Ravielli

93

LET IT FLY!

How to hit the best possible shot from a flyer lie

There are many different lies in the rough. One of the trickiest is the "flyer" lie, and it looks like this: The ball is sitting up in the rough with a few blades of grass behind it. At impact, the grass will prevent the grooves on the clubface from making clean contact with the ball, and as a result, the ball will come out hot with no spin. It will fly and roll much farther.

The most important adjustment you can make is to take less club than you normally would. Next, aim for a closer target that will allow for more distance and roll. For example, if your target from the middle of the fairway would have been the center of the green, aim for the front edge. Hopefully, you'll see your shots cozy up to the pin. *Nancy Lopez*

94

FAULT: "CASTING FROM THE TOP"

Maintain the angle between your left arm and club for more power

One of the sure signs of a swing that's out of control is "casting from the top." When a player tries for extra power, often she has a tendency to flip the club at the start of the downswing rather than maintain a good angle between the left arm and the club. If you can keep this angle until the club enters the hitting area you'll retain the power and force of your swing.

Here's a good way to help ensure that you maintain your wrist cock at the top of your backswing. Begin the transition to the downswing by pulling the club down with the last three fingers of your left hand. That not only will maintain the proper angle, but also will help prevent you from coming over the top on the downswing.

Amy Alcott

A. Ravielli

95

DECIDE AND COMMIT

When it comes to picking the shot and club you're going to hit, don't overthink

Consider the lie, the target and any trouble in your way, but keep it simple. Once you make a decision, focus only on what you need to do—no second-guessing. If you feel nervous or think your swing is getting a little quick, take one more club and swing smoothly.

Annika Sorenstam

96

FRINGE BENEFITS

What happens when an opponent's ball interferes with your line of play

If Player A believes that the ball of Player B might interfere with her play, she may ask that it be lifted. Thus, Player B is required to mark and lift her ball when asked to do so by Player A, regardless of whether it was on or off the green. Here's where it gets interesting: If Player B refuses to comply with a rule affecting the rights of another competitor in stroke play, she can be disqualified. In match play, Player B would lose the hole. *Genger Fahleson*

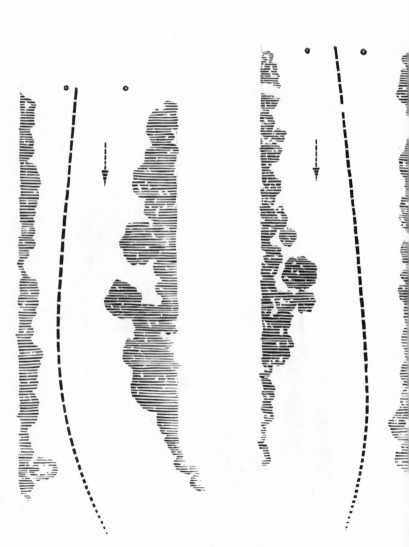

97

MANAGING YOUR TEE BALL

Tee up on the same side of trouble and hit away from it

Playing your tee shot from different positions on the tee depends on how the hole sets up. As a general rule, I tee up on the same side the trouble is and hit away from it. If trouble lurks down the right side, I tee up on the right side, aim down the right side of the fairway, and plan to hit a draw. I wouldn't try to fade the ball over on the left and then have it working towards the trouble. I prefer to work the ball away from the trouble. This way, even if I pull the ball, I'll probably find a safe landing.

Judy Dickinson

98

PRE-SHOT ROUTINE

Do all of your thinking before you swing away

Maintain the same physical and mental routines on every shot. Survey the shot, visualize the shot, take your stance, and make your swing with the same routine in the same cadence every time.

Make sure your routine includes: 1) choosing a target on the fairway; 2) choosing a spot to tee up, usually on the opposite side of the tee from the target; 3) picking out an intermediate target—maybe a leaf or a clump of dirt four or five feet in front of the ball; 4) visualizing the shot and its trajectory; and 5) checking to make sure your alignment is correct. The key is to eliminate the questions before you swing, so your muscle memory will take over. Then, just keep it smooth. *Patty Sheehan*

99

THE REVERSE PIVOT

What causes it, and how to fix it

Whether we like it or not, most of our weight is located in the hip areas—our center of gravity. At least 90 percent of the women we teach move their hips too much to the right in the backswing. When the hips sway to the right, the spine is thrown to the left, causing an incorrect weight movement called the reverse pivot.

Try to control your hips by turning them only 45 degrees, by keeping your left foot closer to the ground in the backswing, and by holding the right leg post in its original address position throughout the backswing. This is called keeping the post. The weight should go to the inside of the right heel on the backswing. You are actually turning around the post.

Peggy Kirk Bell

100

BACK TO TARGET

Try this simple back-swing image for a more complete turn

One reason I'm able to repeat my swing is because I keep it simple. For me, it always comes down to my backswing: If I make a full turn going back, so that my back faces the target, my body unwinds naturally and the ball just gets in the way of my club. If I start to think about my impact position or where my hands are at the finish, then I'm tinkering too much. Don't complicate your swing; keep it simple. *Annika Sorenstam*

AFTERWORD

HAVING THE OPPORTUNITY to see Anthony Ravielli's original scratchboards reminded me how many different talents exist in golf. Each day at *Golf for Women* we have the privilege to work with the women of the LPGA Tour, as well as top amateurs. From instruction to lifestyle, we consider the unlimited variety of women who share a common bond: love of

  the game. Sometimes for fun, sometimes for competition, these diverse women from all walks of life— including film star Jane Seymour, emerging business leader Ivanka Trump, and world-class athlete Annika Sorenstam—can come together on the course.

In *100 Classic Golf Tips from Leading Ladies' Teaching and Touring Pros*, Ravielli's drawings illuminate timeless tips from the archives of *Golf for Women* and *Golf Digest*. Just as his art represents the finest example of mastering the swing or a nuance of the game, the accompanying tips from golf legends— Mickey Wright, Kathy Whitworth, and Nancy Lopez, among others—bring forth wisdom developed over the past century of women's golf.

Wishing you much success and happiness, on and off the course.

Susan Reed Editor in Chief, *Golf for Women*

WOMEN'S GOLF AND FAMILY MEMORIES

WHILE LOOKING THROUGH the archives of
the Ravielli instructional illustrations with my father
and identifying golfers, we came upon an image which
took him back his childhood: Ravielli had apparently
been commissioned to illustrate Blanche Graham Sohl.
Sohl's image brought back memories of his mother, my
grandmother, and her days of golfing at the Scioto Club.

Since its founding in 1916, Scioto Country Club set forth to create a lasting legacy of giving golfers a home and providing an environment to encourage men and women to celebrate the game. Donald Ross set the stage with his masterful design. Once the fairways and greens had matured, like a field of dreams, golfers came from near and far, even across the pond, to play. Scioto hosted the 1926 U.S. Open, with Bobby Jones winning a year prior to his unprecedented four Major victories, and the second Ryder Cup in 1931. It was home to golfing legend Jack Nicklaus. The club was also home to Blanche Sohl, Women's Ohio State Champion, who inspired many of the female athletes.

As a little girl during these years, my grandmother watched her uncle, Neil Postlewaite, actively working to create an exceptional club—a club where she would spend her entire life making friends, marrying, and then raising her family.

As my father reflects, Jack was among the many golfers who would wander over to their house on the way to the course. Coming through the kitchen door, he could always count on finding my grandma ready with a homemade brownie, cinnamon sugar cookie, or the ever-present chocolate chip treat. From there, the boys were off, and grandma was happy to make sure there was more than balls and tees in their golf bags. But she also played as well, showing up

every Tuesday morning for ladies golf. Never mastering the game, always having fun, she enjoyed the camaraderie and never complained as her handicap seemed endlessly stuck in double bogey land.

Ironically, my lifelong friend Jody VanBuren told me recently that it was my grandfather, Dr. Robin Obetz, who as chair of the greens committee in 1964 "liberated women's golf at Scioto." As at most clubs, there were stringent dress codes, especially for women. The Scioto Code of Regulations stated "no peddle pushers, shorts, or any type of slacks allowed." According to Jody, who was a new member at the time, she was in the ladies locker room when all the women were expressing the desire to wear Bermuda shorts. The group nominated Jody to go and model the shorts for the very serious and proper Dr. Obetz. As it turned out, Jody did a great job presenting the women's case. Afterward, she recalls, my grandfather "got up from the lunch table, disappeared, then returned with a yardstick, measuring from the waist to the knee." The new modified dress code was approved from that day forward.

Women's golf, whether at Scioto or other clubs, has had a lasting impact on those who play for fun as well as those who compete. Ravielli, throughout his career, was able to capture women at their best and preserve their technique. *Sports Illustrated* and *Golf Digest* always made sure to recognize the female athlete, and with Ravielli on assignment, women's golf had the sport's greatest artistic master helping them share their secrets of the game.

RAVIELLI REMEMBERED

LOOKING BACK UPON the fateful day several years ago when I stumbled into the second floor of a converted bank building on Madison Avenue in New York, the walls covered with eighteenth- and nineteenth-century paintings, the rooms bursting with every possible period of American and European furnishings, who would have guessed how many lives would change from this spontaneous encounter?

I remember the moment with incredible joy. My memories are filled with the ancient golf bag that first caught my attention, the wooden-shafted putters and clubs strewn everywhere, the gallery owner in his red golf cap putting down the wood floors of his forty-foot entry foyer into a tin cup—and then the amazement of seeing the sketches of Bobby Jones with accompanying text and handwritten notes, the original cover illustration of Ben Hogan for *Five Lessons: The Modern Fundamentals of Golf,* and countless images of golfers, both men and women, captured at their most recognized moment in the swing. I'm still astonished to think that what is considered the Holy Grail of golf instruction illustrations was just a day away from the auction block, to be separated forever. The artist, who was published in *Sports Illustrated*, in *Golf Digest* for four decades, as well as in the most read golf instructional books of the century, was going to fade into history as quietly as he lived his life.

Anthony "Tony" Ravielli was a man of few words. This comes through even in his art. A golfer

looking to master a technique need not read long-winded text, or spend hours listening to endless advice; simply studying a Ravielli illustration offers the lesson in its subject communicated to the artist. Then, it goes without saying, practice, practice, practice. Hit the range, shag the balls, spend time off the practice green, walk the fairways—this is how one becomes a true golfer, and a lover of the game.

Ravielli was able to translate the swing into detailed black line etchings yet keep the illustrations simple and clear thanks to his scratchboard technique

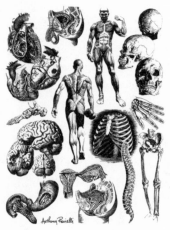

ANTHONY RAVIELLI
scratchboard illustration

79 LOLLY LANE   STAMFORD, CT. 06903   TEL. (203) 322-9011

combined with his keen knowledge of anatomy. Early on, as an artist fascinated with natural science and anatomy, he studied and worked at the American Museum of Natural History and the morgues of Bellevue Hospital in New York, which offered him insight into how the body functioned in athletics.

Ravielli eventually became the go-to artist for anyone interested in visually illustrating their point of view when the human body was involved—whether it was the world's most revered bowler, Don Carter, or international ski sensation Stein Eriksen, or the genius Isaac Asimov, who hired the artist to illustrate *The Human Body*.

Ravielli could dissect any part of the body, removing the layers of skin to show how musculature reacts to the movement. Here, for example, he illustrates Hogan wearing only his signature hat and shoes along with the internal components of the hand for lessons on set up and the grip.

According to his wife Georgia, true to his quiet demeanor Ravielli never wanted to take credit for anything other than the perfection of his technique: "He received tremendous satisfaction from the problem solving associated with the translation of golfers' words and the vision of their technique into art." The pleasure he received came from the internal acknowledgment when he completed an illustration that defined the decisive moment being discussed. Due to his shy nature, one of the most recognized golf teaching techniques—the Hogan plane of glass—almost escaped his name being associated with it. "It truly was a collaboration between Hogan, [Herbert] Wind, and Tony," Georgia states. "The irony is that people remember Hogan as a teacher, Wind as the writer, yet the art created from Tony remained relatively nameless, and it is the art people actually associate with the concept."

Georgia brings up another little known fact about Ravielli: his great sense of humor. "He was extremely serious when it came to his work, but he also loved to play," she says. Occasionally, he would receive an assignment that allowed him to show his sense of humor. Simplicity was at the heart of his work, and he loved to play with items and visuals from everyday life to enhance instruction—carrying a tray of filled glasses to demonstrate balance at the top of the backswing in the

parallel position, or using a broom to show the "sweeping technique" for the initial movement in the backswing, for example.

Ravielli never would have dreamed that his art would have extended to so many levels, and to so many people. His works have influenced decades of golfers, and today they continue to be the backbone of golf instruction. His drawings have permeated the minds—and swings—of millions worldwide. Although his name is only just beginning to be recognized, his art is no longer a forgotten beauty. It is found and forever remembered.

First published in the
United States of America in 2008
by Universe Publishing,
A Division of Rizzoli International Publications, Inc.
300 Park Avenue South
New York, NY 10010
www.rizzoliusa.com

2008 2009 2010 2011 / 10 9 8 7 6 5 4 3 2 1

Design by Opto

Printed in the United States

ISBN-13: 978-0-7893-1596-0

Library of Congress Catalog Control Number:
2008900424